PEEKING INTO THE MILLIONAIRE LIFESTYLE

Unveiling the Luxurious World of Millionaires

By Erick stifler.

TABLE OF CONTENT

Chapter 1

Introduction to the Millionaire Lifestyle

The allure of the millionaire lifestyle has captivated the imagination of people across the globe for centuries. It evokes visions of opulent mansions, luxurious cars, exotic vacations, and the freedom to pursue one's passions without financial constraints.

However, the millionaire lifestyle extends beyond material possessions, encompassing a mindset, values, and habits that contribute to both financial success and personal fulfillment.

In this book, we will delve into the various facets of the millionaire lifestyle, exploring the mindset, key principles, and strategies employed by individuals who have achieved remarkable wealth.

1. The Mindset of Millionaires:

One of the defining characteristics of millionaires is their mindset. They possess a unique perspective on wealth creation, abundance, and success. Instead of succumbing to a scarcity mentality, millionaires embrace an abundance mindset, believing that there are unlimited opportunities for financial growth.

They view money not as a scarce resource but as a tool to create value and enhance their lives and the lives of others.

Moreover, millionaires understand the power of positive thinking and the importance of self-belief.
They cultivate an unwavering belief in their ability to succeed and adopt a proactive approach to problem-solving.
This mindset enables them to overcome obstacles, bounce back from failures, and seize opportunities that come their way.

2. Key Principles of the Millionaire Lifestyle:

Financial Discipline and Planning:
Millionaires prioritize financial discipline
and meticulously plan their financial future.
They understand the significance of
budgeting, saving, and investing wisely.

They live within their means, avoiding
unnecessary debt and frivolous expenses.
Furthermore, millionaires recognize the
importance of diversification and long-term
financial goals, thereby reducing risks and
ensuring sustainable wealth accumulation.

Continuous Learning and Personal Growth:
Millionaires understand that knowledge is
power.

They have a thirst for learning and
self-improvement, constantly expanding
their knowledge in areas such as finance,
entrepreneurship, and personal
development.

They invest time and effort into acquiring new skills, staying up-to-date with industry trends, and networking with like-minded individuals.This commitment to continuous learning enables them to adapt to changing circumstances and capitalize on emerging opportunities.

Entrepreneurial Spirit and Innovation: Many millionaires have achieved their wealth through entrepreneurial ventures.

They possess an innate entrepreneurial spirit, which drives them to identify problems and create innovative solutions.

Millionaires are often risk-takers, willing to step out of their comfort zones and pursue unconventional paths. They understand that entrepreneurship provides the potential for limitless growth and financial freedom.

3. Strategies for Achieving the Millionaire Lifestyle::

Millionaires set clear, specific, and achievable goals. They envision their desired lifestyle and create a roadmap to guide their actions.

By defining their objectives, they are better able to focus their efforts, make informed decisions, and measure their progress. Moreover, they break down their goals into smaller milestones, celebrating each achievement along the way.

Building Multiple Streams of Income:
To achieve the millionaire lifestyle, diversifying sources of income is crucial. Millionaires seek opportunities to generate income from various channels, such as investments, real estate, royalties, and business ventures.
This strategy not only provides financial security but also opens doors for wealth creation and long-term financial stability.

Cultivating a Strong Network:
Successful millionaires recognize the power of connections and actively cultivate a strong network. They surround themselves with like-minded individuals who inspire and challenge them to reach new heights.

By building mutually beneficial relationships, millionaires gain access to valuable resources, mentorship, and opportunities that propel their success.

The millionaire lifestyle extends far beyond material wealth. It is a combination of mindset, principles, and strategies that contribute to financial success and personal fulfillment.

By adopting the mindset of abundance, embracing key principles such as financial discipline and continuous learning, and employing strategies like goal-setting and diversifying income streams, individuals can embark on the path towards the millionaire lifestyle.

It requires dedication, perseverance, and a relentless pursuit of growth and self-improvement. Ultimately, the millionaire lifestyle is not only about accumulating wealth but also about creating a life of purpose, impact, and fulfillment.

Chapter 2

The Mindset of Millionaires

There has been extensive research and analysis on the mindset of millionaires. While no one solution works for everyone, people who have found financial success tend to share a few traits and viewpoints in common. I'll discuss some important facets of millionaires' mindset in this reply, offering details on their thought processes and actions.

1. Vision and Goal-Orientation: People who are millionaires typically have a clear idea of what they want to accomplish and have established specific goals to direct their actions. They look at things in the long run and prioritize wealth accumulation over short-term gains. They are aware that success is a process, and they are prepared to make short-term compromises to accomplish their long-term objectives.

2. Positive and Growth-Oriented Mindset: Millionaires have a mindset that is both positive and growth-oriented. They have faith in their capacity to generate wealth and spot chances where others might see barriers. They do not let setbacks discourage them because they see failures as teaching opportunities. Instead, they see setbacks as chances to develop, modify, and enhance their approaches.

3. Financial Literacy and Lifelong Learning: Millionaires recognize the value of financial literacy and invest in their lifelong learning about wealth creation, investing, and money management.

They stay current with industry trends, consult experts, and base their decisions on knowledge and research. They actively look for opportunities to pick up new knowledge and abilities because they understand that knowledge is a major factor in success.

4. Persistence and Resilience: Successful millionaires persevere in achieving their objectives. They are prepared to put in the required effort and work hard to accomplish their goals because they are aware that success does not happen overnight. Challenges and failures do not easily deter them; instead, they use them as motivation to press on. They persevere in the face of challenges, change course when necessary, and uphold a strong work ethic.

5. Taking Strategic Risks: Wealthy people are not afraid to take strategic risks. They are aware that building wealth frequently entails stepping outside of their comfort zones and making risky investments or business decisions. They do thorough research and analysis before making decisions, however, and avoid taking careless risks in favor of carefully weighing

the benefits and risks of various scenarios. They are aware that taking calculated risks can result in significant rewards.

6. Proactive and Action-Oriented: Successful people who have made a million dollars are proactive and take the initiative to seize opportunities. Instead of waiting for things to happen, they spot opportunities, make a decision, and seize them.

They don't rely too heavily on others to open doors for them because they are self-starters who are prepared to accept responsibility for their success.

7. Surrounding Oneself with Success: Successful people are aware of the impact their surroundings have on their success and mindset. They surround themselves with supportive, motivated, and ambitious people who share their values.
They look for mentors and counselors who can offer advice and motivate them to

achieve greater levels of success. They are aware that the people they surround themselves with can either advance them or hold them back.

8. Generosity and Giving Back: Millionaires frequently have an abundance mindset and think that it is important to give back to society. They understand how their wealth can be used to improve the lives of others and the world they live in.

They give to their communities, participate in charitable endeavors, and practice philanthropy. They are aware that true wealth includes improving the lives of others in addition to achieving financial success.

In summary, millionaires have a mindset that combines vision, optimism, ongoing learning, tenacity, calculated risk-taking, proactive behavior, and surrounding themselves with successful people.

These people have a strong belief in their capacity to generate wealth, and they use their skills, resources, and knowledge to that end. While achieving financial success is frequently the main goal, millionaires also recognize the value of developing personally, giving back to the community, and leaving a lasting legacy.

9. Self-Control and Delayed Gratification: Millionaires have self-control when it comes to their financial management. They are prepared to make short-term sacrifices in exchange for long-term gain because they recognize the value of delaying gratification.

They avoid impulsive purchases and instant gratification, placing a higher priority on saving and investing money. They can consistently and steadily increase their wealth thanks to this discipline.

10. Self-Belief and Confidence: Millionaires have high levels of self-confidence and

confidence in themselves. They have faith in their judgment and confidence in their skills.

They can take calculated risks and take advantage of opportunities because they don't let self-doubt get in the way. They have self-esteem, which attracts opportunities and puts them in a successful position.

11. Flexibility and Adaptability: Millionaires welcome change because they recognize that the business environment is constantly changing.

They are flexible and able to change their approaches and strategies when necessary. They actively seek out new information, keep up with industry trends, and are receptive to novel concepts. They stay ahead of the curve and can successfully navigate difficulties because they are adaptable.

12. Persistence in Creating Multiple Streams of Income: Millionaires frequently understand the value of diversifying their

sources of income. They are aware of the risks involved in having just one source of income.

As a result, they work to develop multiple sources of income, such as stock, real estate, business, or royalty investments. They strengthen their financial foundation and improve their chances of accumulating wealth by diversifying.

13. Adopting a Long-Term Wealth Mindset: Millionaires have a long-term wealth mindset and look beyond short-term financial gains. They put a lot of effort into building wealth that will endure economic ups and downs and offer security to both current and future generations. They make strategic choices that are in line with their long-term financial objectives and invest in assets that increase in value over time.

14. Accepting Failure and Learning from Mistakes: Millionaires view failure

differently. Instead of seeing it as a failure, they see it as a chance for development and learning.

 They accept failure as a necessary learning experience and are aware that it is a necessary step on the road to success. When they experience failure or make mistakes, they reflect on the event, draw conclusions, and make changes to better their future performance.

15. Constant Goal-Setting and Achievement: Millionaires do not stop after achieving a certain level of wealth and consider themselves successful. They continually set new objectives and work to fulfill them.

They are aware that development and improvement are ongoing processes. They maintain momentum and avoid complacency by setting and achieving goals, which keeps them motivated and encourages them to keep going for excellence.

16. Concentrate on Creating Value: Millionaires frequently have a mindset that is focused on generating value for others. They identify needs and come up with creative solutions to meet them through their investments, services, or goods.

They create prosperous businesses and financial edifices by concentrating on adding value to people's lives. They put quality service and having a positive impact first, which helps them succeed in the long run.

17. Creating a Strong Work Ethic: Millionaires have a strong work ethic and are prepared to make the sacrifices required to accomplish their objectives. They are aware that dedication, perseverance, and consistency are necessary for success.

They are prepared to go above and beyond, put in a lot of effort, and make compromises to achieve their goals. They stand out for having a strong work ethic, which also helps explain their financial success.

In conclusion, the mindset of millionaires includes perseverance, confidence, flexibility, adaptability, diversification, long-term thinking, acceptance of failure, ongoing goal-setting, value creation, a strong work ethic, and more.

It is a multifaceted mindset that combines character traits, money management techniques and a dedication to lifelong learning.

Chapter 3

Wealth Creation Strategies

The term "wealth creation strategies" refers to the various techniques and plans that people and organizations use to gradually build up and expand their financial resources.

These tactics seek to boost earnings, make money, and accumulate assets to create long-term wealth and financial security. Here are some essential methods for generating wealth:

1. Saving and budgeting: Setting aside a regular amount of your income and adhering to a strict spending plan are two fundamental tactics for building wealth. You can build up savings over time that you can invest to create wealth by setting aside a portion of your income and spending money sensibly.

2. Investing: Putting your money into different financial instruments or assets in the hope of making a profit is an effective wealth-creation strategy. Stocks, bonds, real estate, mutual funds, and exchange-traded funds (ETFs) are typical investment options.

Investment diversification across various asset classes can help to reduce risk and increase returns.

3. Entrepreneurship: Establishing and growing a profitable business can be an important strategy for accumulating wealth. Entrepreneurs can make a significant profit and amass wealth by spotting opportunities, developing cutting-edge goods or services, and developing a scalable business model. However, careful planning, market research, and risk management are necessary for entrepreneurship.

4. Trading on the stock market: Making money by actively participating in the stock

market is possible. In stock trading, shares are bought and sold to profit from price swings. To make wise investment decisions, you need knowledge, research, and risk management abilities.

5. Real estate investment: Purchasing real estate, such as homes, businesses, or rental properties, can be a successful wealth-building strategy. Real estate investments have the potential to increase in value over time and provide regular income through rental payments.

6. Passive Income Streams: Creating multiple passive income streams is a well-liked wealth creation technique. This can include income from investments or online businesses, dividends from stocks, interest from bonds or savings accounts, royalties from intellectual property, and rental income from real estate.

7. Education and skill development: Investing in education and skill

development can greatly increase your chances of creating wealth and increasing your earning potential. Gaining specialized knowledge, going to college, or honing your skills in industries that are in high demand can open doors to higher-paying employment opportunities or help you launch successful businesses.

8. Financial Planning and Wealth Management: Maximizing wealth creation can be accomplished by enlisting the assistance of qualified financial advisors and conducting thorough financial planning.

Financial planners can offer advice on risk management, retirement planning, tax planning, estate planning, and investment strategies while also tailoring plans to specific goals and situations.

9. Long-Term Investing: Making long-term investments can be a smart way to build wealth. Compounding returns can be

obtained by investing in reputable businesses or diversified index funds, and by keeping a long-term perspective, you may be able to withstand momentary market volatility.

10. Continuous Learning and Adaptation: As market conditions change, new opportunities materialize, and technologies advance, wealth creation strategies change over time. Therefore, for long-term wealth creation, adopting a mindset of continuous learning, keeping up with market trends, and adapting your strategies accordingly can be crucial.

It's crucial to remember that your risk tolerance, financial objectives, and time horizon should all be taken into account when choosing wealth creation strategies. Getting expert guidance from wealth managers or financial advisors can help you customize these strategies for your unique situation and goals.

Chapter 4

Managing Finances Like a Millionaire

Adopting certain behaviors and techniques that can assist people in achieving financial independence and accumulating long-term wealth is necessary for managing money like a millionaire. While there is no surefire way to become a millionaire, there are some common strategies and ways of thinking that many wealthy people use to manage their finances successfully. Here are some important factors to think about:

1. Budgeting and expense tracking: Millionaires are aware of the value of budgeting and expense tracking. They develop a thorough budget that details their income and expenses, enabling them to allocate money wisely and spot opportunities to cut costs. They can maintain accountability and make the necessary changes to their spending patterns with the aid of expense tracking.

2. Prioritizing saving and investing a portion of their income is a trait of millionaires. They frequently adhere to the "pay yourself first" maxim, which means setting aside a portion of their income for savings and investments before doing anything else.

They concentrate on accumulating an emergency fund for unforeseen costs and make investments in a variety of financial products to increase their wealth over time, including stocks, bonds, real estate, and businesses.

3. Living within their means: Despite having a high income, millionaires may not always spend it all. Instead, they frequently avoid making unnecessary or extravagant purchases to live within their means.

They are conscious of their spending patterns and put long-term financial objectives ahead of temporary indulgences.

They can quickly amass wealth if they continue to lead a frugal lifestyle.

4. Diversifying your sources of income: Millionaires frequently have several different sources of income. They are aware of the value of diversification in protecting themselves from unforeseen events or financial downturns.

They may make money through a variety of sources, including investments, business endeavors, rental income from real estate, royalties, and side jobs. Their earning potential is increased and a safety net is created by having multiple sources of income.

5. Lifelong learning and financial literacy: Millionaires are aware of the importance of financial literacy for long-term success. They put time and effort into learning about wealth management, tax planning,

investment strategies, and personal finance. They keep up with market developments and, when necessary, consult with financial professionals for advice. They are better able to make wise decisions and steer clear of costly errors thanks to this knowledge.

6. Long-term outlook: Millionaires approach their finances with a long-term perspective. They establish specific financial objectives and lay out a plan to achieve them. They are aware that accumulating wealth requires time and patience, and they are prepared to postpone immediate gratification in exchange for greater rewards down the road. When obstacles arise, they bounce back quickly and see them as opportunities for growth rather than failures.

7. Surrounding themselves with the right network: Millionaires frequently associate with people who have similar values and aspirations in terms of money.
They look for mentors, join networking organizations, and participate in communities where they can absorb knowledge from the experiences of others. Having a strong network behind them can help them succeed financially by offering advice, inspiration, and useful connections.

It's crucial to remember that managing money like a millionaire requires self-control, dependability, and flexibility. Because every person's financial journey is different, it's important to customize these strategies according to each person's specific needs and objectives. People can take significant steps toward financial independence and improve their chances of amassing wealth over time by adopting these behaviors and mindsets.

8. Minimizing debt and using credit responsibly: Millionaires are aware of the risks associated with debt and work to keep it to a minimum. They attempt to pay off high-interest debts, like credit card balances, as soon as they can.

They also strategically use credit, using low-interest loans for investments that have a chance of paying off, like real estate or business endeavors. They take good care of their debt-to-income ratio and make on-time payments to keep their credit score high.

9. Tax optimization: Wealthy people are aware of the negative effects taxes may have on their assets. They collaborate with tax experts or financial advisors to legally optimize their tax planning strategies. They make use of tax-advantaged savings accounts, capital gains tax planning, and retirement accounts as investment vehicles.

They can maximize the amount of wealth they accumulate and keep more of their income by reducing their tax obligations.

10. Philanthropy and giving back: Many millionaires recognize the value of supporting charitable causes and giving back to their communities. They allocate a portion of their wealth for charitable donations and incorporate philanthropy into their financial plans. This not only contributes to having a positive effect, but in some places, it may also have tax advantages.

11. Risk management and insurance are priorities for millionaires when it comes to safeguarding their assets and reducing possible risks. They are aware of the value of having insurance protection for their businesses, homes, lives, and health. They regularly check their insurance policies to make sure they have enough coverage and

adjust them as necessary in light of their shifting needs.

12. Estate planning: To safeguard their wealth and ensure a seamless transfer of assets to their beneficiaries, millionaires frequently engage in thorough estate planning.

They collaborate with experts in estate planning to draft wills, trusts, and other legal documents that reduce estate taxes, preserve privacy, and establish precise guidelines for asset distribution.

13. Regular financial review and adjustment. Periodically, they evaluate their financial progress, evaluate the performance of their investments, and make any necessary strategy adjustments. As a result, they can stay on track with their objectives and adjust their course as needed to take into account shifting market conditions or personal circumstances.

14. Mindset and perseverance: In the end, managing money like a millionaire necessitates having a positive outlook and the willpower to get past obstacles. A growth mindset, which is the conviction that one can constantly improve one's financial situation, is common among millionaires.

Even in the face of obstacles, market volatility, or economic downturns, they maintain their composure, self-control, and fortitude.

Never forget that managing money like a millionaire involves more than just building wealth; it also entails achieving financial security, peace of mind, and the freedom to follow one's passions and objectives.

Financial choices must be made in a way that is consistent with one's values and priorities while keeping the long term in mind.

Chapter 5

Living the High Life

For a very long time, people from all walks of life have been fascinated by the idea of living the high life as a millionaire. Through the media, popular culture, and societal perceptions, the image of opulence, luxury, and indulgence frequently associated with millionaires is perpetuated.

The appeal and realities of a millionaire living a high life are examined in this essay, along with the experiences, advantages, and difficulties they encounter.

Privileges of the High Life: Financial freedom is one of the main privileges enjoyed by millionaires living the high life. They have enough money to be able to afford the best that life has to offer. They have no restrictions on their ability to indulge in their passions and desires, whether it be buying expensive hobbies, rare items, or collecting art. Living the high life, millionaires have access to exclusive networks and social circles that offer chances for networking, business partnerships, and per connections that can increase their wealth and influence.

Expensive Experiences and Possessions:
The pursuit of extravagant possessions is a sign of high life. Millionaires may opt to own opulent homes in desirable locations, complete with cutting-edge amenities and breathtaking views. They might own an array of luxurious vehicles, yachts, private planes, or even their islands.

Millionaires living the high life enjoy extraordinary experiences in addition to material possessions. They might travel in first class, stay in opulent resorts, partake in extreme sports, attend exclusive events, and have access to exclusive clubs and entertainment venues.

Living the High Life and Finding Personal Fulfillment:
For some millionaires, finding personal fulfillment comes from leading a high life. It stands for the culmination of their efforts, aspirations, and achievements. A feeling of accomplishment and satisfaction can come from being able to take pleasure in the results of their labor.

The high life may also offer opportunities for horizon-widening exposure to various experiences, personal development, and cultural enrichment. Additionally, enjoying a luxurious lifestyle can enhance one's sense of social acceptance and a positive self-image.

Despite the allure, there are difficulties and things to think about when living a high life as a millionaire. Risk analysis, investment strategies, and careful financial planning are all necessary for managing significant wealth. Maintaining a luxurious lifestyle comes with a lot of pressure to keep up appearances and live up to expectations from society, which can make stress levels rise. Additionally, the desire for privacy and exclusivity may lead to a feeling of loneliness and make it difficult to build sincere relationships.

Social perceptions and criticism:
The wealthy class' extravagant lifestyle frequently draws attention from the media and public. Some see it as a demonstration of extravagant wealth and extravagance that highlights social injustice and wealth inequality.

Critics contend that millionaires enjoying the good life ought to use their resources to address important global issues, support charitable causes, or advance social change. It is important to understand that not all millionaires who live opulently disregard their social obligations, as many of them take part in philanthropic and charitable endeavors.

Balance and Purpose:
For millionaires living a high life, achieving a sense of balance and purpose is essential. While living a lavish lifestyle can be rewarding, it's important to avoid becoming overly materialistic and to put personal well-being, meaningful connections, and the pursuit of passions before anything else.

Some millionaires find fulfillment in giving back to society, whether it be by starting foundations, making charitable contributions, or serving as mentors to others. An experience of a high life that is more satisfying and meaningful can result from developing a sense of purpose that goes beyond material possessions.

Millionaire living is a complex experience that goes beyond opulent experiences and material possessions. It entails a way of thinking and living that covers a range of topics, such as financial responsibility, self-care, and personal development.

Millionaires who are living the high life have the chance to invest in their personal development and self-improvement. They can invest time and money into learning new things, developing new skills, and pursuing their intellectual or artistic interests. They can widen their horizons and develop a more in-depth understanding of the world by continuing to learn through participation in seminars, workshops, or higher education.

Another crucial element of the high life is self-care. Millionaires frequently have busy schedules and a lot of responsibilities, so it's important to put their health first. They have the financial means to partake in pursuits that enhance both physical and psychological well-being, such as spa visits, exercise routines, and wellness retreats. Millionaires who take care of themselves can maintain the drive and concentration required to lead their fast-paced lives successfully.

Responsible Wealth Management:
Millionaires must responsibly manage their wealth in addition to enjoying the luxuries of the high life.
Creating sound investment strategies that protect and increase their assets, entails close collaboration with financial advisors and industry professionals.

 By investing in various businesses, start-ups, or charitable endeavors, they can diversify their portfolio and ensure the long-term financial stability of both themselves and future generations.

Furthermore, contributing to society through philanthropic and charitable

endeavors is a component of responsible wealth management.
Millionaires who lead opulent lives can positively influence the world by donating to causes they are passionate about.

They can create foundations, give to already-existing charities, or take part in social entrepreneurship to address urgent issues like poverty, healthcare, education, and environmental preservation.

Finding Meaning and Fulfillment:
Despite the abundance of material goods that come with the high life, real meaning, and fulfillment can only be found by looking beyond material things.

Many millionaires understand that contentment and happiness cannot be solely derived from outside forces. They look for contentment in close friendships, kinships, and a sense of direction.

Building and maintaining sincere bonds with loved ones, such as family and friends, becomes crucial. Millionaires who are living the high life can make time for their loved ones, fostering close relationships and shared experiences.

 They can also use their resources to organize events, trips, and celebrations that deepen ties and leave enduring impressions.

Finding your purpose in life is another crucial component of living it up. Millionaires frequently engage in charitable activities that fit with their values and passions.

They can significantly improve the lives of others by addressing societal challenges with their wealth and influence. This sense of purpose gives their high-life journey a deeper meaning and enhances their sense of fulfillment.

Comes With Its Fair Share of Pressures: Navigating Challenges and Maintaining

Authenticity. Stress can be greatly increased by societal expectations, the need to constantly project success, and the worry about losing wealth. Millionaires must overcome these obstacles by staying true to who they are and what they believe in.

In the face of external pressures, authenticity must be preserved. It entails maintaining personal integrity, remaining grounded, and resisting temptations to indulge in excess or superficiality. Millionaires are more likely to feel true happiness and contentment if they can strike a balance between their lofty life goals and their guiding principles.

Chapter 6

Entrepreneurship and Business Success

Entrepreneurship and business success go hand in hand, but being successful in business can be difficult and requires several different factors to come together. Here are some essential guidelines and tactics that can promote entrepreneurship and commercial success:

1. Clarity of Vision and Passion: Successful business owners are passionate about their concepts and have a clear vision for their company.
They have a burning desire to realize their vision and are prepared to put forth the necessary effort and dedication to do so.

2. Market Research: It's essential to carry out in-depth market research before starting a business. Understanding the target

market, determining customer needs, and assessing the competition are all necessary for this. This knowledge aids business owners in creating goods or services that satisfy consumer needs and give them a competitive edge.

3. Effective Planning: Success depends on creating a well-thought-out business plan. The company's objectives, strategies, target market, financial projections, and other information are detailed in a business plan. It acts as a road map, assisting business owners in making wise choices and maintaining focus on their goals.

4. Adaptability: Successful businesspeople are flexible because the business environment is ever-changing. They are receptive to fresh perspectives, flexible in their approach, and quick to change course when necessary. For long-term success, it is essential to be

adaptable and responsive to market trends and customer feedback.

5. Effective Leadership: Strong leadership is essential for moving a company forward. Strong leadership qualities are possessed by successful business owners, including the capacity to inspire and motivate their team, make difficult choices, and take calculated risks. They cultivate an environment at work that is supportive of growth, innovation, and teamwork.

6. Putting Together a Talented Team: Entrepreneurs can't succeed on their own. It is essential to assemble a talented and committed team. The secret to achieving business objectives is creating a positive work environment and selecting employees with the appropriate qualifications and experience.

7. Customer Focus: It's important to put the customer at the center of your business.

Successful businesspeople are aware of their clients' needs and work hard to satisfy them with exceptional goods and services. To ensure customer satisfaction and loyalty, they cultivate strong relationships, pay attention to customer feedback, and make ongoing improvements to their products.

8. Financial Management: Successful business operations depend on sound financial management. Entrepreneurs must gain a thorough understanding of their financial situation, including cash flow, sales, and costs. They manage costs efficiently, make wise financial decisions, and look for funding or investment opportunities when necessary.

9. Marketing and branding: To reach target consumers and raise brand awareness, effective marketing and branding strategies are crucial. Successful business owners invest in marketing initiatives to build a strong brand presence, interact with

customers, and set themselves apart from rivals.

10. Continuous Learning: Entrepreneurs who are successful embrace continuous learning because the business environment is dynamic. They keep up with industry trends, seek mentorship and advice, attend conferences, and make investments in their own personal and professional development.

Keep in mind that failure and setbacks are inevitable parts of the entrepreneurial and business journey. Entrepreneurs can, however, improve their chances of creating profitable businesses by putting these ideas and methods into practice.

Chapter 7

Network And Relationship Building

Both personally and professional,networking and relationship building are crucial skills. They entail making and maintaining connections with others to widen your social and professional networks, promote collaborations, and build rapport. Whether you want to launch a business, advance your career, or simply widen your horizons, networking, and developing relationships can lead to new opportunities and offer invaluable support.

When it comes to networking and relationship building, keep the following important factors in mind:

1. Authenticity: Establishing lasting connections requires authenticity. Be sincere and show that you care about others.

Genuineness builds trust and lays the groundwork for a solid relationship.

2. Active listening: Effective networking requires careful listening. Ask insightful questions, show that you are genuinely interested in what others are saying, and show that you respect their experiences and viewpoints. Active listening promotes stronger connections and rapport-building.

3. Networking has a two-way exchange of benefits. Look for chances to help others, whether it be by imparting knowledge, offering support, or arranging introductions. You establish a reputation for being dependable and supportive by being kind and helpful.

4. Wide-ranging connections: Don't restrict yourself to a single sector or group. Cast a wide net and look for connections with people from different industries, backgrounds, and levels of expertise.

Diverse connections allow for the cross-fertilization of ideas, the introduction of new opportunities, and the offering of new perspectives.

5. Presence both online and offline: In the current digital era, online networking is crucial. Connect with like-minded people by using social media platforms, professional networks like LinkedIn, and industry-specific forums. Don't undervalue the influence of in-person interactions, though. To make new friends and develop rapport, go to conferences, trade shows, and meetups.

6. Follow up and maintain relationships: Developing relationships don't stop after the first encounter or exchange. Whether it's a personalized email, a phone call, or a coffee meetup, follow up with your contacts. By checking in, sharing pertinent information, or connecting them with others who may be of interest, you can stay

involved and develop those relationships over time.

7. Provide and accept feedback: Positive criticism is essential for both professional and personal development. Be receptive to criticism and ready to offer it when necessary. You can improve your relationships and show that you're committed to everyone's development by fostering a culture of feedback.

8. Long-term perspective: Networking and relationship building are not about instant gratification or business-to-business deals. Consider the long term and devote time and energy to growing your relationships. Develop lasting friendships that will support you on your journey by standing the test of time.

Time, effort, and a sincere interest in others are necessary for networking and relationship building. You can build a strong network that can provide support, direction, and opportunities for growth on both a personal and professional level by fostering authentic connections, actively engaging with others, and maintaining relationships.

Chapter 8

Personal Growth and Well-being

A fulfilling and balanced life requires both personal development and well-being. They entail increasing one's knowledge and abilities, fostering constructive relationships, and looking after one's physical, emotional, and mental well-being. To advance one's well-being and personal development, concentrate on the following areas:

1. Self-reflection and self-awareness: Spend some time thinking about your goals, values, and beliefs. You can better understand yourself and make decisions that are in line with your true self when you are self-aware.

2. Constant learning: Develop a growth mindset and look for opportunities to learn and pick up new information and abilities. This can be accomplished through formal

education, reading books, taking courses, going to workshops, or engaging in intellectually challenging hobbies.

3. Setting goals: Create specific, attainable goals for your career, relationships, health, and personal growth, among other areas of your life. Divide them up into smaller, more manageable steps, and continuously monitor your progress. Setting goals offers motivation and direction.

4. Healthy routines: Make regular exercise, a healthy diet, and enough sleep a priority for your physical well-being. Mental and emotional health is directly impacted by physical health. Include activities that you find enjoyable and that are good for your body.

5. Mindfulness and stress management: Use mindfulness practices to cultivate a sense of presence and lower stress levels, such as deep breathing exercises or meditation.

Find healthy coping mechanisms for stress, such as taking up a hobby, spending time in nature, or asking loved ones for help.

6. Creating wholesome connections: Surround yourself with uplifting, upbeat people who support your development. Spend time developing deep connections with others and nurturing meaningful relationships. The importance of healthy relationships to overall well-being cannot be overstated.

7. Emotional intelligence: You can improve your emotional intelligence by effectively understanding and controlling your own emotions as well as those of others.

Relationship management, conflict resolution, and emotional wellness are all made easier with the help of emotional intelligence.

8. Self-care: Give self-care pursuits that will recharge and revitalize your top priority. This could entail taking up a hobby, developing self-compassion, using relaxation techniques, or getting help from a professional when necessary. For personal development, it's essential to look after your mental and emotional well-being.

9. A positive outlook and gratitude: Develop a positive outlook by emphasizing gratitude and changing your perspective to see the good things in life. Regularly expressing gratitude can boost happiness and general well-being.

10. Giving back: Take part in deeds of kindness and support the welfare of others and your neighborhood. Volunteering or providing assistance to others not only makes you feel good inside, but it also fosters personal growth by broadening your empathy and perspective.

Keep in mind that the road to personal development and well-being never ends. It's critical to be patient with yourself, acknowledge small accomplishments, and modify your strategy as you advance.

Chapter 9

Overcoming Challenges and Maintaining Success

A millionaire's success is frequently the result of perseverance, wise choices, and overcoming obstacles along the way. A different set of abilities and approaches are needed to sustain success and overcome new challenges. Here are some pointers for overcoming obstacles and keeping your millionaire status:

1. Adopt a growth mindset: A growth mindset is essential for ongoing professional and personal growth. This way of thinking acknowledges that difficulties present chances for development. Consider setbacks as stepping stones to success rather than failure, and look for ways to advance and adjust.

2. Maintain focus on your objectives: Establish distinct, long-term objectives and

divide them into manageable steps. Keep a clear vision of what you want to accomplish, and review and revise your goals as needed regularly. Avoid letting temporary setbacks or outside noise divert your attention from your priorities.

3. Develop your resilience. Resilience is the capacity to overcome hardship and keep a positive outlook. Create coping mechanisms and approaches to handle stress, failures, and unforeseen difficulties.

Create a network of supportive mentors, counselors, and like-minded people around you who can offer direction and inspiration when things are difficult.

4. Continue to learn and adapt: Because the world is ever-changing, successful people must be knowledgeable and adaptable. By participating in conferences, seminars, and workshops, reading books, and keeping up with industry trends, you can invest in your

own professional and personal growth. Accept innovative approaches, techniques, and concepts that can keep you on the cutting edge.

5. Effectively manage risks: Success frequently requires taking calculated risks. To safeguard your wealth and maintain long-term success, it's crucial to evaluate and manage risks effectively. Make informed decisions based on a balanced risk-reward analysis by conducting in-depth research, consulting experts, diversifying your investments, and following these steps.

6. Develop a strategic network of contacts: Success depends on having a solid network of contacts. Spend time with people who uplift and challenge you and who share your values. Look for mentors who are willing to mentor others and who can offer advice and support. Join forces with like-minded professionals, go to industry gatherings, and take advantage of networking opportunities.

7. Remain humble and grounded: Despite your success, it's crucial to maintain your composure. Keep in mind your beginnings and the sacrifices you made to get where you are.
Respect and empathy should be shown toward others, and you should always be willing to learn from others. Positivity, trust, and new opportunities are all cultivated by upholding a humble attitude.

8. Give back to society: Possibilities to change the world for the better arise from success. Think about being charitable and supporting causes that are in line with your values. Charity work not only benefits those in need, but it also gives people a sense of fulfillment and purpose that goes beyond material success.

9. Take care of yourself: Your physical, emotional, and mental health should not be sacrificed for success. Make self-care a

priority, keep a healthy work-life balance, and use stress-reduction methods. Make time for hobbies, exercise, time with loved ones, and engaging in enjoyable and relaxing activities.

10. Maintain your moral compass: Success can occasionally result in temptations or moral conundrums. It's critical to uphold your integrity and remain true to your core beliefs. Remember that long-term success is built on a foundation of trust, honesty, and ethical behavior, and make decisions by your moral compass.

Keep in mind that obstacles are a natural part of every journey, and that success requires ongoing effort and adaptation. You can overcome challenges and maintain your millionaire lifestyle by remaining determined, strong, and committed to your values.

Chapter 10

Embracing the Millionaire Lifestyle: Tips and Advice

Adopting certain behaviors, attitudes, and money management techniques can help you become wealthy and lead fulfilling lives. This is what it means to live the millionaire lifestyle. Here are some pointers and recommendations to aid you on your travels:

1. Create a Wealth Mindset: Develop a positive attitude toward wealth and money. Believe that you can build wealth through hard work, wise investments, and perseverance. You have the power to create abundance.

2. Establish Specific Financial Goals: Specify your financial goals and design a plan to reach them. Establish SMART goals specific, measurable, attainable, relevant, and time-bound for both your short and long-term objectives.

3. Establish a Budget and Keep Track of Expenses: Setting up a budget is essential for efficient money management. To find out where your money is going, keep track of your income and expenses. Determine where you can reduce wasteful spending and put more money toward investments and savings.

4. Save and Invest Wisely: Make saving a top priority and work to consistently set aside some of your income. Create an emergency fund to pay for unforeseen costs.

Additionally, educate yourself on the various investment options available, including stocks, real estate, mutual funds, and business startups. Increase potential returns and reduce risk by diversifying your investments.

5. Always Learn New Things: Commit to lifelong learning. Keep up with the most recent developments in business, investing, and finance. Read books, go to seminars or workshops, and pay attention to key figures in business and finance. You'll be better able to make wise financial decisions the more information you gain.

6. Surround Yourself with People Who Share Your Views: Join forces with those who share your philosophy and objectives. Being around ambitious, driven people can be a source of motivation, support, and useful connections. Participate in industry events, networking groups, or online forums with like-minded people.

7. Take Reasonable Risks: Taking Reasonable Risks is a common component

of wealth building. Be prepared to venture outside of your comfort zone and investigate opportunities with a high profit potential. However, before making any significant financial decisions, always do your homework and exercise due diligence.

8. Maintain Discipline and Persistence: Building wealth takes time and requires discipline and persistence.
Even when things are difficult, remain committed to your goals. Accept delayed gratification and refrain from impulsive purchases. Never forget that accumulating wealth takes time and requires patience.

9. Develop Healthy Habits: Wealth includes both material abundance and general well-being. Maintain your physical and mental well-being.

Live a balanced lifestyle, engage in regular exercise, get enough sleep, and give yourself priority. Your success in all facets of life can be attributed to having a healthy body and mind.

10. Give Back and Show Gratitude: As you prosper financially, keep in mind to help those in need and give back to the community.
Be thankful for the opportunities that come your way and cultivate gratitude for the things you have accomplished. Giving can give your millionaire lifestyle a sense of fulfillment and purpose.

Remember that leading a millionaire lifestyle involves more than just having material possessions; it also involves achieving financial freedom and building an abundant, happy, and impactful life.
 It calls for commitment, ongoing learning, and a positive outlook. Start using these suggestions right away and take pleasure in achieving your financial objectives.